By W. H. Auden

THE ORATORS

AN ENGLISH STUDY

W·H·AUDEN

THE ORATORS

AN ENGLISH STUDY

RANDOM HOUSE   NEW YORK

As a rule, when I re-read something I wrote when I was younger, I can think myself back into the frame of mind in which I wrote it. *The Orators*, though, defeats me. My name on the title-page seems a pseudonym for someone else, someone talented but near the border of sanity, who might well, in a year or two, become a Nazi.

The literary influences I do remember more or less. The sections entitled *Argument* and *Statement* contain, as Eliot pointed out to me in a letter, 'undigested lumps of St-John Perse'. I had recently read his translation of *Anabase*. The stimulus to writing *Journal of an Airman* came from two sources, Baudelaire's *Intimate Journals*, which had just been translated by Christopher Isherwood, and a very dotty semi-autobiographical book by General Ludendorff, the title of which I have forgotten. And over the whole work looms the shadow of that dangerous figure, D. H. Lawrence the Ideologue, author of *Fantasia of the Unconscious* and those sinister novels *Kangaroo* and *The Plumed Serpent*.

The central theme of *The Orators* seems to be Hero-worship, and we all know what that can lead to politically. My guess to-day is that my unconscious motive in writing it was therapeutic, to exorcise certain tendencies in myself by allowing them to run riot in phantasy. If to-day I find 'Auden with play-ground whistle', as Wyndham-Lewis called him, a bit shy-making, I realise that it is precisely the schoolboy atmosphere and diction which act as a moral criticism of the rather ugly emotions and ideas they are employed to express. By making the latter juvenile, they make it impossible to take them seriously. In one of the Odes I express all the sentiments with which his followers hailed the advent of Hitler, but these are rendered, I hope, innocuous by the fact that the Führer so hailed is a new-born baby and the son of a friend.

W. H. A.

THE ORATORS

AN ENGLISH STUDY

Prologue

B Y L A N D S C A P E reminded once of his mother's figure
The mountain heights he remembers get bigger and bigger:
With the finest of mapping pens he fondly traces
All the family names on the familiar places.

Among green pastures straying he walks by still waters;
Surely a swan he seems to earth's unwise daughters,
Bending a beautiful head, worshipping not lying,
'Dear' the dear beak in the dear concha crying.

Under the trees the summer bands were playing;
'Dear boy, be brave as these roots', he heard them saying:
Carries the good news gladly to a world in danger,
Is ready to argue, he smiles, with any stranger.

And yet this prophet, homing the day is ended,
Receives odd welcome from the country he so defended:
The band roars 'Coward, Coward', in his human fever,
The giantess shuffles nearer, cries 'Deceiver.'

BOOK I

THE INITIATES

I

Address for a Prize-Day

COMMEMORATION. COMMEMORATION. What
does it mean? What does it mean? Not what does
it mean to them, there, then. What does it mean to us,
here, now? It's a facer, isn't it, boys? But we've all got to
answer it. What were the dead like? What sort of people
are we living with now? Why are we here? What are we
going to do? Let's try putting it in another way.

Imagine to yourselves a picked body of angels, all quali-
fied experts on the human heart, a Divine Commission,
arriving suddenly one day at Dover. After some weeks in
London, they separate, one passing the petrol pumps along
the Great North Road, leaving the dales on his left hand,
to take all rain-wet Scotland for his special province, one
to the furnace-crowded Midlands, another to the plum-rich
red-earth valley of the Severn, another to the curious delta-
like area round King's Lynn, another to Cornwall where
granite resists the sea and our type of thinking ends, and
so on. And then when every inch of the ground has been
carefully gone over, every house inspected, they return to the

[7]

Capital again to compare notes, to collaborate in a complete report, which made, they depart as quietly as they came. Beauty of the scenery apart, would you not feel some anxiety as to the contents of that report? Do you consider their statistics as to the average number of lost persons to the acre would be a cause for self-congratulation? Take a look round this hall, for instance. What do you think? What do you think about England, this country of ours where nobody is well?

All of you must have found out what a great help it is, before starting on a job of work, to have some sort of scheme or plan in your mind beforehand. Some of the senior boys, I expect, will have heard of the great Italian poet Dante, who wrote that very difficult but wonderful poem, *The Divine Comedy*. In the second book of this poem, which describes Dante's visit to Purgatory, the sinners are divided into three main groups, those who have been guilty in their life of excessive love towards themselves or their neighbours, those guilty of defective love towards God and those guilty of perverted love. Now this afternoon I want, if I may, to take these three divisions of his and apply them to ourselves. In this way, I hope, you will be able to understand better what I am driving at.

To start with, then, the excessive lovers of self. What are they like? These are they who even in childhood played in their corner, shrank when addressed. Lovers of long walks, they sometimes become bird-watchers, crouching for hours among sunlit bushes like a fox, but prefer as a rule the big cities, living voluntarily in a top room, the curiosity of their landlady. Habitués of the mirror, famous readers, they fall in love with historical characters, with the unfortunate queen, or the engaging young assistant of a great detective, even with the voice, of the announcer, maybe, from some foreign broadcasting station they can never identify; unable to taste pleasure unless through the rare coincidence of naturally diverse events, or the performance of a long and intricate ritual. With odd dark eyes like windows, a lair for engines, they pass, suffering more and more from cataract or deafness, leaving behind them diaries full of incomprehensible jottings, complaints less heard than the creaking of a wind pump on a moor. The easiest perhaps for you to recognise. They avoid the study fire; at games they are no earthly use. They are not popular. But isn't it up to you to help? Oughtn't you to warn them then against tampering like that with time, against those strange moments they look forward to so? Next time you see one sneaking from the field to develop photographs, won't you ask if you can come too? Why not go out together next Sunday; say, casually, in a wood: 'I suppose you realise you are fingering the levers that control eternity!'

Then the excessive lovers of their neighbours. Dare-devils of the soul, living dangerously upon their nerves. A rich man taking the fastest train for the worst quarters of eastern cities; a private school-mistress in a provincial town, watching the lights go out in another wing, immensely passionate. You will not be surprised to learn that they are both heavy smokers. That one always in hot water with the prefects, that one who will not pass the ball; they are like this. You call them selfish, but no, they care immensely, far too much. They're beginning to go faster. Have you never noticed in them the gradual abdication of central in favour of peripheral control? What if the tiniest stimulus should provoke the full, the shattering response, not just then but all the time. It isn't going to stop unless you stop it. Daring them like that only makes them worse. Try inviting them down in the holidays to a calm house. You can do most for them in the summer. They need love.

Next the defective lovers. Systems run to a stand-still, or

like those ship-cranes along Clydebank, which have done nothing all this year. Owners of small holdings, they sit by fires they can't make up their minds to light, while dust settles on their unopened correspondence and inertia branches in their veins like a zinc tree. That tomato house blown down by the autumn gales they never rebuilt. Wearers of soiled linen, the cotton wool in their ears unchanged for months. Often they are collectors, but of what? Old tracts, brackets picked up on the road, powders, pieces of wood, uncatalogued, piled anyhow in corners of the room, or hidden under tea-stained saucers. Anaemic, muscularly undeveloped and rather mean. Without servants. Each hour bringing its little barrowful of unacted desires, mounting up day after day, week after week, month after month, year after year has made a slag heap miles high shutting out air and sun. It's getting rather smelly. The effort required for clearance will be immense. Dare they begin? Well, you've got to show them they'd jolly well better dare. Give them regular but easy tasks and see that they do them properly. Hit them in the face if necessary. If they hit back you will know they are saved.

Last and worst, the perverted lovers. So convincing at first, so little apparent cause for anxiety. A slight proneness to influenza, perhaps, a fear of cows, traits easily misunderstood or dismissed. Have a good look at the people you know; at the boy sitting next to you at this moment, at that chum of yours in the Lower School. Think of the holidays, your father, the girl you met at that dance. Is he one? Was she one? Yes, they are charming, but they've lost their nerve. Pray God, boys, you may not have to see them as they will be not so very long from now. 'What have you been up to?' you'd think; 'What did you ask for to be given that?' Faces in suffering so ugly they inspire feelings only of disgust. Their voice toneless, they stoop, their gait wooden like a galvanised doll so that one involuntarily exclaims on meeting, 'You really oughtn't to be out in weather like this.' In some a simple geometrical figure can arouse all the manifestations of extreme alarm. Others, haters of life, afraid to die, end in hospitals as incurable cases. These are they who when the saving thought came shot it for a spy. Unable to sleep at nights, they look at watches as the train passes, pushed struggling in towards a protracted death-bed, attended by every circumstance of horror, the hard death of those who never have and never could be loved.

Who have done this? There must be several here. Yes I can see some already. There you sit, who smooth sick pillows, devoted as lice, yet have no day-dreams: wince at no curse, are never ill, put kindness, words and sleekness in. You're going to have friends, you're going to bring up children. You're going to be like this for ever, all the time, more terrible than the bursting of the bolted door or the exhausting adverse wind of dreams.

Now, boys, I want you all to promise me that you'll never be like that. Are you just drifting or thinking of flight? You'd better not. No use saying 'The mater wouldn't like it,' or 'For my part I prefer to read Charles Lamb'. Need I remind you that you are no longer living in Ancient Egypt? Time's getting on and I must hurry or I shall miss my train. You've got some pretty stiff changes to make. We simply can't afford any passengers or skrimshankers. I should like to see you make a beginning before I go, now, here. Draw up a list of rotters and slackers, of proscribed persons under headings like this. Committees for municipal or racial improvement—the headmaster. Disbelievers in the occult—the school chaplain. The bogusly cheerful—the games master. The really disgusted—the teacher of modern languages. All these have got to die

[11]

without issue. Unless my memory fails me there's a stoke hole under the floor of this hall, the Black Hole we called it in my day. New boys were always put in it. Ah, I see I am right. Well look to it. Quick, guard that door. Stop that man. Good. Now, boys, hustle them, ready, steady—go.

II

Argument

Lo, I a s k u l l s h o w y o u, exuded from dyke when no pick was by pressure of bulbs: at Dalehead a light moving, lanterns for lambing. Before the forenoon of discussion, as the dawn-gust wrinkles the pools, I waken with an idea of building.

Speak the name only with meaning only for us, meaning Him, a call to our clearing. Secret the meeting in time and place, the time of the off-shore wind, the place where the loyalty is divided. Meeting of seven, each with a talent.

On the concrete banks of baths, in the grassy squares of exercise, we are joined, brave in the long body, under His eye. (Their annual games under the auspices of the dead.) Our bond, friend, is a third party.

Smile inwardly on their day handing round tea. (Their women have the faces of birds.) Walking in the mountains we were persons unknown to our parents, awarded them little, had a word of our own for our better shadow. Crossing ourselves under the arch of a bridge, we crucified fear.

Crofter, leader of hay, working in sweat and weathers, tin-streamer, heckler, blow-room major, we are within a vein's distance of your prisoned blood. Stranger who cannot read our letters, you are remembered.

Rooks argue in the clump of elms to the left. Expect what dream above the indented heel, end-on to traffic, down the laurelled drive?

At the frontier getting down, at railhead drinking hot tea waiting for pack-mules, at the box with the three levers watching the swallows. Choosing of guides for the passage through gorges.

The young mother in the red kerchief suckling her child in the doorway, and the dog fleaing itself in the hot dust. Clatter of nails on the inn's flagged floor. The hare-lipped girl sent with us as far as the second turning. Talk of generals in a panelled room translated into a bayonet thrust at a sunbrowned throat, wounds among wheat fields. Grit from the robbers' track on goggles, a present from aunts. Interrogation of villagers before a folding table, a verbal trap. Execution of a spy in the nettled patch at the back of the byre. A tale of sexual prowess told at a brazier and followed by a maternal song. The fatty smell of drying clothes, smell of cordite in a wood, and the new moon seen along the barrel of a gun. Establishment of a torpedo base at the head of the loch; where the bye-roads meet, a depot for tractors, with sliding doors. Visit to a tannery in the hill-village where the stream runs under the houses; to the mine with obsolete machinery, an undershot wheel, steam pipes in the open, swaddled in sacking. Designs for the flow sheet of a mill. Sound of our hammers in the solemn beat of a quarry, and the packing of labelled specimens in japanned boxes. Theories inter-relating the system of feudal tenure with metabolic gradients, and arguments from the other side of the lake on the formation of hanging valleys, interrupted by the daughter of the house with a broken doll. Writing reports for Him in the copper-green evenings. (Trunks, caught by the grapnel, dragged inert towards the spurting saw, ewers of warm milk, the sugary layer under the rind, and pipe-line clamped to the rock and at the tiny post-office, His word waiting.)

If it were possible, yes, now certain. To meet Him alone on the narrow path, forcing a question, would show our unique knowledge. Would hide Him wounded in a cave, kneeling all night by His bed of bracken, bringing hourly an infusion of bitter herbs; wearing His cloak receive the mistaken stab, deliver his message, fall at his feet, He gripping our moribund hands, smiling. But never for us with notebooks there, a league of two or three waiting for low water to execute His will. The tripod shadow falls on the dunes. World of the Spider, not Him.

Rook shadows cross to the right. A Schoolmaster cleanses himself at half-term with a vegetable offering; on the north side of the hill, one writes with his penis in a patch of snow 'Resurgam'.

Going abroad to-day? Under a creaking sign, one yellow leg drawn up, he crows, the cock. The dew-wet hare hangs smoking, garotted by gin. The emmet looks at sky through lenses of fallen water. Sound of horns in the moist spring weather, and the women tender. I feel sorry for you, I do.

Girls, it is His will just now that we get up early. But watching the morning dredger, picking the afternoon fruit, wait; do not falsify our obedience. When we shuffle at night late round up-country stoves, although in waders, a dance of males, it is your hour; remember. It is your art just now against the inner life. Parting by hangars we are sorry, but reborn.

Wrap gifts in clothes, prepare a present for a simpler nation. A heliograph seen from below, a camera with smuggled lenses: a soured drink for the tongue, a douche for the unpopular member, a dream dirt-cheap for the man of action. Leave the corks behind as warning of wires, let the shafts be fenced as before, leave ordinary kindness.

Going abroad to-night? The face lit up by the booking-clerk's window. Poetry of the waiting-room. Is it wise, the short adventure on the narrow ship? The boat-train dives accomplished for the hoop of the tunnel; over the derne cutting lingering, its white excreta. Too late: smelling the first sea-weed we may not linger. The waving handkerchiefs recede and the gulls wheel after, screaming for scraps. Throb of turbines below water, passing the mud islands, the recurrent light. Past. Handrail, funnel, oilskins, them, His will. The lasting sky.

11

Remember not what we thought during the frost, what we said in the small hours, what we did in the desert. Spare us, lest of our own volition we draw down the avalanche of your anger: lest we suffer the tragic fate of the insects:

O Four Just Men, spare us.

From the immense bat-shadow of home; from the removal of land-marks: from appeals for love and from the comfortable words of the devil:

O Dixon Hawke, deliver us.

From all opinions and personal ties; from pity and shame; and from the wish to instruct:

O Sexton Blake, deliver us.

From all nervous excitement and follies of the will; from the postponed guilt and the deferred pain; from the oppression of noon and from the terror in the night:

O Bulldog Drummond, deliver us.

From the encroaching glaciers of despair, from the drought that withers the lower centres; from the star Wormwood, and from the death by burning:

O Panther Grayle, deliver us.

By the flash of insight in the rears; by the slow influence of natural scenery; by the phrase in the book and by the word overheard on the platform:

O Poirot, deliver us.

In the moment of vision; in the hour of applause; in the place of defeat; and in the hour of desertion:

O Holmes, deliver us.

For those who dance in the capitals; for those who handle a saw; those who discuss the problem of style and those aware of the body; for those who have done everything and those who dare not begin:

O Cat with the Fiddle, hear us.

For those who cannot go to bed; for those in dormitories; for those in pairs; for those who sleep alone:

O Bull at the Gate, hear us.

For the devoted; for the unfaithful; for those in whom the sexual crisis is delayed; for the two against one, and for the Seven against Thebes:

O Goat with the Compasses, hear us.

For the virgin afraid of thunder; for the wife obeyed by her husband; for the spinster in love with Africa:
> O Bear with the Ragged Staff, hear us.

For those who grow by division; for those who protest their innocence; for those who decline to die:
> O Blue Boar, hear us.

For those who borrow and for those who lend; for those who are shunned on the towpath; for those regarded in their households as saints:
> O Swan with the Two Necks, hear us.

For sunbathers; for those who dress soberly; for those who expect to be respected, and for those who have been taught to adore:
> O White Horse, hear us.

For those determined to suffer; for those who believe they can control the weather:
> O Jack Straw from your castle, hear us.

For those capable of levitation; for those who have days of collapse; for those whose impulses are negative:
> Fair Maid of Kent, hear us.

For those who elect to live in the bower; for those on the hill; for those who return to the epoch of the poisoner:
> O Man laden with Mischief, hear us.

For those who take vows of silence; for those who do not; for those who visit churches after the death of sons:
> O Marquis of Granby, hear us.

For all parasites and carrion feeders, for the double rose and for domesticated animals:
O Green Man, hear us.

And that it may please thee to calm this people:
George, we beseech thee to hear us.

I I I

Came one after a ruined harvest, with a school-room globe, a wizard, sorry. From the nipping North Righteousness running. But where that warm boy of the summer château? Found on wet roads early this morning, patches of oil, the face of an avenger, downwards. Speech of worn tools in a box, thoughts from the trap.

Sound of guns in the city, the voice of the demonstrator, 'Gentlemen, to-morrow we shall tie the carotid.' What memory of self-regard from the locked room, shaken by lorries, from the depressed areas?

Suspicion of one of our number, away for week-ends. Catching sight of Him on the lawn with the gardener, from the upper rooms of a house. His insane dislike of birds. His fondness for verbal puzzles. Friendly joking converting itself into a counterplot, the spore of fear. Then in the hot weeks, the pavement blistering and the press muzzled, the sudden disaster, surprising as a comic turn. Shutting the door on the machines, we stood in the silence, thinking of nothing. (Murder of a rook by weasels.) Some taking refuge in thankful disillusion, others in frank disbelief, the youngest getting drunk. Hysterical attempts of two women to reach him. The slow seeping in of their sly condolences, of the mass hatred of the villas. A child's sense of failure after burning a slug in a candle.

Daylight, striking at the eye from far-off roofs, why did you blind us, think: we who on the snow-line were in love with death, despised vegetation, we forgot His will; who came to us in an extraordinary dream, calming the plunging dangerous horses, greeting our arrival on a reedy shore. His sharing from His own provisions after the blizzard's march. The thrashing He gave the dishonest contractor who promised marvels in an old boy's tie. The old peasant couple's belief in His magical powers. His ability to smell a wet knife at a distance of half a mile. His refusal to wear anything but silk next to His skin. His reverent stories of the underpaid drunken usher who taught Him all. His tale of the Three Sorb Trees. His words after we had failed Him at the Roman bridge.

Love, that notable forked one, riding away from the farm, the ill word said, fought at the frozen dam, transforms itself to influenza and guilty rashes. Seduction of a postmistress on the lead roof of a church-tower, and an immature boy wrapping himself in a towel, shamed at the public baths. From these stony acres, a witless generation, plant-like in beauty.

On the steps of His stone the boys play prisoner's base, turning their backs on the inscription, unconscious of sorrow as the sea of drowning. Passage to music of an unchaste hero from a too-strict country. March, long black piano, silhouetted head; cultured daughter of a greying ironmaster, march through fields. The hammer settles on the white-hot ingot. The telescope focuses accurately upon a recent star. On skyline of detritus, a truck, nose up. Loiterer at carved gates, immune stranger, follow. It is nothing, your loss. The priest's mouth opens in the green graveyard, but the wind is against it.

III

Statement

M EN PASS through doors and travel to the sea, stand grouped in attitudes of play or labour, bending to children, raising equal's glass, are many times together, man with woman. To each an award, suitable to his sex, his class and the power.

One charms by thickness of wrist; one by variety of positions; one has a beautiful skin, one a fascinating smell. One has prominent eyes, is bold at accosting. One has water sense; he can dive like a swallow without using his hands. One is obeyed by dogs; one can bring down snipe on the wing. One can do cart wheels before theatre queues; one can slip through a narrow ring. One with a violin can conjure up images of running water; one is skilful at improvising a fugue; the bowel tremors at the pedal-entry. One amuses by pursing his lips; or can imitate the neigh of a randy stallion. One casts metal in black sand; one wipes the eccentrics of a great engine with cotton waste. One jumps out of windows for profit. One makes leather instruments of torture for titled masochists; one makes ink for his son out of oak galls and rusty nails. One makes bedsteads, adorned with carvings, at the request of friends. One in a red-brick villa makes designs for a bridge, creates beauty for a purpose. One is eloquent, persuades committees of the value of spending: one announces weddings in a solemn voice. One is told secrets at night, can stop a young girl biting her nails. One can extirpate a goitre with little risk. One can foretell the migrations of mackerel; one can distinguish the eggs of sea-birds. One is a lightning calculator; he is a young one. One is clumsy but amazes by his knowledge of time-tables. One delivers buns in a van, halting at houses. One can emend a mutilated text; one can estimate the percentage of moisture in a sample of nitre. One decorates a room for a lady in black and silver; one manufactures elephant drums for a circus. One has an extraordinary capacity for organising study circles. One fosters snowdrops in a green bowl. One does nothing at all, but is good.

Summon. And there passed such cursing his father, and the curse was given him.

I I

Do not listen at doors.

On lawns in flannels, in garages, in golf clubs, talking, starting slightly at the shooting, the small disaster on the limit-less plain, returning from matches after the streets are lit, who can protest at the words from the other room.

One slips on crag, is buried by guides. One gets cramp in the bay, sinks like a stone near crowded tea-shops. One is destroyed in his bath, the geyser exploding. One is arrested for indecent exposure. One suffers from an intestinal worm; men remark on his paleness. One believes himself to be two persons, is restrained with straps. One cannot remember the day of the week. One is impotent from fear of the judgment. One pays for foolishness with the loss of land. One loses his job for an error in long division. One drinks alone in another country. One repels by unsightly facial eruptions; one is despised for wearing stiff collars. The wife of one is unfaithful with schoolboys. One is bullied by an elder sister; one is disappointed in his youngest son.

Always think of the others.

One is saved from drowning by a submerged stake. One healed by drinking from a holy well. One is honoured by a countess with a gift of grapes. One is hailed as the master by monthly reviews. One is known in his club as 'the Skipper'. One discovers in middle age his talent for painting. One is a hero, covered with medals, is greeted by bands. One wins a battle through a change in the weather. One has a unique collection of indigenous insects. One is promoted for his suggestions respecting overhead charges. One makes a fortune out of a locking device for lifts. One receives a grant from a fund for research; one is invited to give a course of lectures on a philosophical subject. One discovers a new variety of sneezewort; it shall be called by his name. The mayorship of one is commemorated by a public lavatory at the cross-roads. One is famous after his death for his harrowing diary.

Have seen the red bicycle leaning on porches and the cancelling out was complete.

III

An old one is beginning to be two new ones. Two new ones are beginning to be two old ones. Two old ones are beginning to be one new one. A new one is beginning to be an old one.

Something that has been done, that something is done again by someone. Nothing is being done but something being done again by someone.

Life is many; in the pine a beam, very still; in the salmon an arrow leaping the ladder. The belly receives; the back rejects; the eye is an experiment of the will. Jelly fish is laziest, cares very little. Tape-worm is most ashamed; he used to be free. Fish is most selfish; snake is most envious, poisoned within; bird is most nervous; he is shot for his spirit. Eagle is proudest. Bull is stupidest, oppressed by blood. Insect is most different; he multiplies for another reason; he is not with us.

The man shall love the work; the woman shall receive him as the divine representative; the child shall be born as the sign of the trust; the friend shall laugh at the joke apparently obscure. The boy and the girl shall not play together; they shall wait for power; the old shall wait in the garden, happy for death. The leader shall be father; he shall protect from panic; the people shall reverence the carved stone under the oak-tree. The muscular shall lounge in bars; the puny shall keep diaries in classical Greek. The soldier shall say 'It is a fine day for hurting'; the doctor shall speak of death as of a favourite dog. The glutton shall love with his mouth; to the burglar love shall mean 'Destroy when read'; to the rich and poor the sign for 'our money'; the sick shall say of love 'It's only a phase'; the psychologist, 'That's easy'; the bugger, 'Be fair'. The censor shall dream of knickers, a nasty beast. The murderer shall be wreathed with flowers; he shall die for the people.

Sun is on right, moon on left, powers to earth. The action of light on dark is to cause it to contract. That brings forth.

IV

Letter to a Wound

T H E   M A I D has just cleared away tea and I shall not be disturbed until supper. I shall be quite alone in this room, free to think of you if I choose and believe me, my dear, I do choose. For a long time now I have been aware that you are taking up more of my life every day, but I am always being surprised to find how far this has gone. Why, it was only yesterday, I took down all those photographs from my mantelpiece—Gabriel, Olive, Mrs. Marshall, Molim, and the others. How could I have left them there like that so long, memorials to my days of boasting? As it is, I've still far too many letters. (Vow. To have a grand clearance this week—hotel bills—bus tickets from Damascus, presentation pocket-mirrors, foreign envelopes, etc.)

Looking back now to that time before I lost my 'health' (Was that really only last February?) I can't recognise myself. The discontinuity seems absolute. But of course the change was really gradual. Over and over again in the early days when I was in the middle of writing a newsy letter to M, or doing tricks in the garden to startle R. and C., you showed your resentment by a sudden bout of pain. I had outbursts, wept even, at what seemed to me then your insane jealousy, your bad manners, your passion for spoiling things. What a little idiot I was not to trust your more exquisite judgment, which declined absolutely to let me go on behaving like a child. People would have tried to explain it all. You would not insult me with pity. I think I've learned my lesson now. Thank you, my dear. I'll try my hardest not to let you down again.

Do you realise we have been together now for almost a year? Eighteen months ago, if anyone had foretold this to me I should have asked him to leave the house. Haven't I ever told you about my first interview with the surgeon? He kept me waiting three quarters of an hour. It was raining outside. Cars passed or drew up squeaking by the curb. I sat in my overcoat, restlessly turning over the pages of back numbers of illustrated papers, accounts of the Battle of Jutland, jokes about special constables and conscientious objectors. A lady came down with a little girl. They put on their hats, speaking in whispers, tight-lipped. Mr. Gangle would see me. A nurse was just coming out as I entered, carrying a white-enamelled bowl containing a pair of scissors, some instruments, soiled swabs of cotton wool. Mr. Gangle was washing his hands. The examination on the hard leather couch under the brilliant light was soon over. Washing again as I dressed he said nothing. Then reaching for a towel turned, 'I'm afraid,' he said. . . .

Outside I saw nothing, walked, not daring to think. I've lost everything, I've failed. I wish I was dead. And now, here we are, together, intimate, mature.

Later. At dinner Mrs. T. announced that she'd accepted an invitation for me to a whist-drive at the Stewarts' on Wednesday. 'It's so good for you to get out in the evenings sometimes.

You're as bad as Mr. Bedder.' She babbled on, secretly disappointed, I think, that I did not make more protest. Certainly six months ago she couldn't have brought it off, which makes me think what a great change has come over us recently. In what I might call our honeymoon stage, when we had both realised what we meant to each other (how slow I was, wasn't I?) and that this would always be so, I was obsessed (You too a little? No?) by what seemed my extraordinary fortune. I pitied everybody. Little do you know, I said to myself, looking at my neighbour on the bus, what has happened to the little man in the black hat sitting next to you. I was always smiling. I mortally offended Mrs. Hunter, I remember, when she was describing her son's career at Cambridge. She thought I was laughing at her. In restaurants I used to find myself drawing pictures of you on the bottom of the table mats. 'Who'll ever guess what that is?' Once, when a whore accosted me, I bowed, 'I deeply regret it, Madam, but I have a friend.' Once I carved on a seat in the park 'We have sat here. You'd better not.'

Now I see that all that sort of thing is juvenile and silly, merely a reaction against insecurity and shame. You as usual of course were the first to realise this, making yourself felt whenever I had been particularly rude or insincere.

Thanks to you, I have come to see a profound significance in relations I never dreamt of considering before, an old lady's affection for a small boy, the Waterhouses and their retriever, the curious bond between Offal and Snig, the partners in the hardware shop on the front. Even the close-ups on the films no longer disgust nor amuse me. On the contrary they sometimes make me cry; knowing you has made me understand.

It's getting late and I have to be up betimes in the morning. You are so quiet these days that I get quite nervous, remove the dressing. No I am safe, you are still there. The wireless this evening says that the frost is coming. When it does, we know what to expect, don't we? But I am calm. I can wait. The surgeon was dead right. Nothing will ever part us. Goodnight and God bless you, my dear.

Better burn this.

BOOK II

JOURNAL
OF AN AIRMAN

Journal of an Airman

A SYSTEM ORGANISES ITSELF, if interaction is undisturbed. Organisation owes nothing to the surveyor. It is in no sense pre-arranged. The surveyor provides just news.

The effect of the enemy is to introduce inert velocities into the system (called by him laws or habits) interfering with organisation. These can only be removed by friction (war). Hence the enemy's interest in peace societies.

Nothing shows the power of the enemy more than that while the fact that a state of tension seeks to relieve itself, seems to us perfectly obvious, an orderly arrangement, the natural result of such an effort, is inexplicable to us without introducing first causes and purposive ends.

The second law of thermodynamics—self-care or minding one's own business.

But—

(1) It is a sure sign of a busybody if he talks of *laissez-faire*.

(2) Self-care is not to be confused with self-regard. Self-care is care-free. Self-regard is the treating of news as a private poem; it is the consequence of eavesdropping.

Note—Self-regard, in origin a mere accident of overcrowding, like haemophilia is a sex-linked disease. Man is the sufferer, woman the carrier. 'What a wonderful woman she is!' Not so fast: wait till you see her son.

A Sure Test.

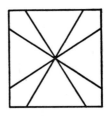

FIG. 1

Give the party you suspect the above figure and ask him to pick out a form from it.

If he pick out either of the two crosses below (Fig. 2) you

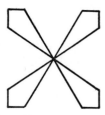 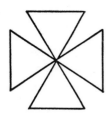

FIG. 2

may accept him as a friend, but if he chooses such a form

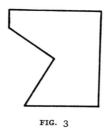

FIG. 3

as Fig. 3 it is wiser to shoot at once.

THE ENEMY IS A LEARNED NOT A NAÏVE OBSERVER

Note Naïve observation—insight.
Introspection   —spying.

The Circle.

FIG. 4

There is a centre and a circumference, and between them is awareness of interdependence—sympathy.

The enemy attempts to disturb this awareness by theories of partial priority.

The Two Circles.

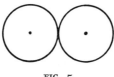

FIG. 5

Between circumference and circumference—awareness of likeness—kindness. Between centre and centre, awareness of difference—love.

THE AIRMAN IS THE AGENT OF THIS CENTRAL AWARENESS

Note 1—The relation between the centres of circles lying on the same axis—ancestor worship. This has nothing to do with history, which is the circle's after-image of itself exploited for private ends.

The true ancestral line is not necessarily a straight or continuous one. Take a simple biological analogy, black and white colour, with white recessive to black.

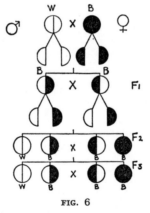

FIG. 6

In the F_3 generation the true ancestor of the pure white is his uncle of his great-grandfather.

My mother's dislike of my uncle, the people's satisfaction at crashes. 'If the Lord had intended people to fly He'd have given them wings', compared with their day-dreams of looping the loop, the falling leaf, dragging their chum from blazing fuselage—signs of a mixed character. Most people mixed characters—the two-faced, the obscure and amazed, the touchline admirers.

Note 2—The aeroplane has only recently become necessary, owing to the progress of enemy propaganda, and even now not for flying itself, but as a guarantee of good faith to the people, frightened by ghost stories, the enemy's distorted vision of the airman's activities.

Vadill of Uirafirth, Stubbo, Smirnadale, Hammar and Sullom, all possible bases: particularly at Hubens or Gluss. Survey to be completed by Monday.

At Grind of the Navir to-day, watching skuas.

> You are a man, or haven't you heard
> That you keep on trying to be a bird?

Of the enemy as philosopher. Talking of intellect-will-sensation as real and separate entities. The Oxford Don: 'I don't feel quite happy about pleasure.'

> We have brought you, they said, a map of the country;
> Here is the line that runs to the vats,
> This patch of green on the left is the wood,
> We've pencilled an arrow to point out the bay.
> No thank you, no tea; why look at the clock.
> Keep it? Of course. It goes with our love.

We shall watch your future and send our love.
We lived for years, you know, in the country,
Remember at week-ends to wind up the clock.
We've wired to our manager at the vats.
The tides are perfectly safe in the bay
But whatever you do don't go to the wood.

There's a flying trickster in that wood,
And we shan't be there to help with our love.
Keep fit by bathing in the bay,
You'll never catch fever then in the country.
You're sure of a settled job at the vats
If you keep their hours and live by the clock.

He arrived at last; it was time by the clock,
He crossed himself as he passed the wood;
Black against evening sky the vats
Brought tears to his eyes as he thought of their love;
Looking out over the darkening country
He saw the pier in the little bay.

At the week-ends the divers in the bay
Distracted his eyes from the bandstand clock;
When down with fever and in the country
A skein of swans above the wood
Caused him no terror; he came to love
The moss that grew on the derelict vats.

And he has met sketching at the vats
Guests from the new hotel in the bay;
Now curious following his love,
His pulses differing from the clock,
Finds consummation in the wood
And sees for the first time the country.

[36]

Sees water in the wood and trees by the bay,
Hears a clock striking near the vats;
This is your country and the home of love.

❖   ❖   ❖

The terrible rat-courage of the enemy. The stout clergyman at our hotel estimating on the back of an envelope the height of the waterfall for the hydraulic engineer.

❖   ❖   ❖

The Enemy as Observer.

His remarks, like those of invalids and precocious children, half-true. His accuracy of description of symptoms compared with his prescription.

'The dog is sick. You see, the hind legs are paralysed. We must get him to walk. Give him a tablespoonful of this arsenic three times a day.' But, doctor, he is suffering from arsenical poisoning.

The antithesis between the passions and reason. The passions are nothing, but the unreal parts as seen by his learned reason (see Fig. 1) of the unity of passion of which nothing can be said but that it is the effort of a thing to realise its own nature. (*N.B.*, however, that the whole has its *real* parts.)

Man miserable without diversion. But diversion is human activity. A man doing nothing is not a man.

Their extraordinary idea that man's only glory is to think.

The misery of a dispossessed king. Who should know that better than the usurper?

The enemy's sense of humour—verbal symbolism. Private associations (rhyming slang), but note that he is serious, the associations are constant. He means what *he* says.

Practical jokes consist in upsetting these associations. They are in every sense contradictory and public, *e.g.* my bogus lecture to the London Truss Club. Derek's seduction of Mrs. Solomon by pretending to have been blessed by the Pope.

❖ ❖ ❖

We leave to-morrow. Uncle Sam is arranging the final sing-song with all the assurance of a non-airman. Catching the largest fish, sieving the funniest story for the ladies, abrogating to oneself the right of feeding the hotel gull, such are the sole manifestations reserved for the spirit when all the risks are known. After tea Bob and Stan, the boy fishermen, will give an exhibition of Japanese wrestling on the floor of the lounge. Community singing of war-time songs will lull for a moment all awareness of lost contracts. At dinner an imaginary telegram of regret from a guest who has left the hotel to die may amuse. In the hall a Highland reel will, of course, be attempted, lit up by pocket torches fetched hurriedly from the bedrooms. Yes, but all the time distant but distinct as the eyepiece image in field-glasses, the thought 'What is to be done? Punch was mistaken; we ought never to have come.' Trapped. Gangrene has already set in.

Only once here, quite at the beginning, and I put it back. Uncle Sam, is he one too? He has the same backward-bending thumb that I have. I wonder. It's going to be all right. Courage. The daily exercise of the will in trivial tasks.

The Airman's Alphabet

ACE—   Pride of parents
                        and photographed person
                        and laughter in leather.

[38]

BOMB—	Curse from cloud and coming to crook and saddest to steeple.
COCKPIT—	Soft seat and support of soldier and hold for hero.
DEATH—	Award for wildness and worst in the west and painful to pilots.
ENGINE—	Darling of designers and dirty dragon and revolving roarer.
FLYING—	Habit of hawks and unholy hunting and ghostly journey.
GAUGE—	Informer about oil and important to eye and graduated glass.
HANGAR—	Mansion of machine and motherly to metal and house of handshaking.
INSTRUMENT—	Dial on dashboard and destroyer of doubt and father of fact.
JOYSTICK—	Pivot of power and responder to pressure and grip for the glove.

KISS—

Touch taking off
and tenderness in time
and firmness on flesh.

LOOPING—

Flying folly
and feat at fairs
and brave to boys.

MECHANIC—

Owner of overalls
and interested in iron
and trusted with tools.

NOSE-DIVE—

Nightmare to nerves
and needed by no one
and dash toward death.

OBSERVER—

Peeper through periscope
and peerer at pasture
and eye in the air.

PROPELLER—

Wooden wind-oar
and twisted whirler
and lifter of load.

QUIET—

Absent from airmen
and easy to horses
and got in the grave.

RUDDER—

Deflector of flight
and flexible fin
and pointer of path.

STORM—

Night from the north
and numbness nearing
and hail ahead.

TIME—	Expression of alarm and used by the ill and personal space.
UNDERCARRIAGE—	Softener of shock and seat on the soil and easy to injure.
VICTIM—	Corpse after crash and carried through country and atonement for aircraft.
WIRELESS—	Sender of signal and speaker of sorrow and news from nowhere.
X—	Mark upon map and meaning mischief and lovers' lingo.
YOUTH—	Day-dream of devils and dear to the damned and always to us.
ZERO—	Love before leaving and touch of terror and time of attack.

Three signs of an airman—practical jokes—nervousness before taking off—rapid healing after injury.

Of the Enemy.

> His collar was spotless; he talked very well,
> He spoke of our homes and duty, and we fell.

Three kinds of enemy walk—the grandiose stunt—the melancholic stagger—the paranoiac sidle.

Three kinds of enemy bearing—the condor stoop—the toad stupor—the robin's stance.

Three kinds of enemy face—the June bride—the favourite puss—the stone in the rain.

Three kinds of enemy eye—the lobster—the boot-button—the submarine.

Three kinds of enemy hand—the marsh—the claw—the dead yam.

Three kinds of enemy clothing—fisherman's pockets—Dickens' waistcoats—adhesive trousers.

Three enemy traits—refusal to undress in public—proficiency in modern languages—inability to travel back to the engine.

Three enemy occupations—playing cards—collecting—talking to animals.

Three terms of enemy speech—I mean—quite frankly—speaking as a scientist, etc.

Three signs of an enemy letter—underlining—parentheses in brackets—careful obliteration of cancelled expressions.

Three enemy questions—Am I boring you?—Could you tell me the time?—Are you sure you're fit enough?

Three enemy catchwords—insure now—keep smiling—safety first.

Three enemy don'ts—don't kiss your baby on the mouth—don't lean out of the carriage window—don't miss this.

Three signs of an enemy country—licensed hours—a national art—nursery schools.

Three signs of enemy house—old furniture—a room called the Den—photographs of friends.

Three warnings of enemy attack—depression in the mornings—rheumatic twinges—blips on the face.

Three symptoms in convalescence—nail-biting—nightmares—short-sight.

Three results of an enemy victory—impotence—cancer—paralysis.

Three counter attacks—complete mastery of the air—ancestor worship—practical jokes.

Monday—Interviewed A about his report.
Tuesday—Pamphlet dropping in Bridgenorth area.
Wednesday—Address at Waterworm College.
Thursday—The Hollies, 7.30.
Friday—See M about the gin to be introduced into the lemonade at the missionary whist-drive.
Saturday—Committee meeting.
Sunday—Break up the Mimosa's lecture on blind flying.

As I thought, A tells me they have been in Kettlewell and most of the outlying farms. A doesn't believe they intend to move before October, which should give us time if only B will move. We know for a fact that tanks are being built at Cockshirt Forge. Can't B see what this means?

Trains keep stopping, regular as dogs, by certain posts. The red dormitory wing of the Academy extrudes a succession of white and black particles which, obedient to laws of attraction and repulsion, quickly assume group patterns, and caught by a northerly current, stream slowly toward the green square. Nurse-maids pause on the esplanade for mutual investigations. The band is leaving the Winter Gardens by an emergency exit. A lady has fainted. Time for lunch. There isn't going to be very much lunch unless you all wake up. The group snapped at the fifth tee against a background of Scotch firs, frowning, conscious of their pipes, cellular underwear, the train whistle in the valley, the tall capless one in the back row deliberately half-hidden, are taken for ambassadors. In the crowded marquee near the front windows the vicar presents the beautiful spy with a handsome eight-day clock, the first prize in the ladies' croquet competition, signs for a registered package brought him by the gardener, with a nickel-plated fountain pen, the gift of his parishioners after twenty years of services. 'A treaty has been arranged,' say the people, and are reassured. The agents smile for a moment then turn back to their charming companions.

Another is afraid and would be safe. Every day his journeys to escape the danger extend further, get more and more dangerous. Circling anxiously for a landing over icy tundras, firing the last drum against frenzied tribes, he can remember a time when a five-minute walk to an aunt's house was quite sufficient. On maps to his red-ink line crossing and re-crossing, sweeps ever wider, to end in a cross marking his approximate position when the last wireless was received, or to be stopped by heart failure at a branch line station among kindly but inconvenienced officials.

But are there not after all some houses to which all this does not apply? Cases of immunity, queer to research, but quite authentic?

Here a home, rather than name which the enemy will employ any circumlocution; there a figure he will cross the street to avoid, assume an interest in a barber's window rather than meet that incorruptible eye. The Hollies, for instance, their most intrepid would steer clear of though disobeying the most urgent order. So far I have said nothing to E. How could he understand a danger more remote from him than the crouching of a sabre-tooth tiger for a Bronze-Age huntsman, or the unsheathing of a knife in a Shanghai bar?

By October:

All Siskens to be replaced by Bulldogs.
3 Short Gunards for reconnaissance.
2 Vickers 163 for troop conveyance.
3 Gloucester s.s.lg for fast fighting.
1 Moth trainer fully equipped for advanced training.
Secure Harvey for first-aid classes.
Darling to replace ffennell (who is perfectly useless) at Hawes.
HURRY. NO MORE GRATE GAZING.

Dawn 13,000 ft. Shadows of struts falling across the cockpit. Perfect calm, light, strength. Yesterday positively the last time. Hands to remember please, always.

Continuity and Discontinuity.

Both true. Continuity in that the *existence* of a whole results from the sum of its parts. Discontinuity in that its *nature* cannot be *inferred* from theirs. The enemy's two waves of attack.

(1) Flux-mongers (shock-troops for destruction).

(2) Order-doctrinaires (establishment of martial law).

The latter of course do not admit collusion into the former, claim rather to come as redeemers.

One must draw the line somewhere. Theory of numbers. Dedekind's section. Not to confuse the real line with that drawn for personal convenience, to remember the margin of safety. By denying the existence of the real line, the enemy offers relief, at a price, from their own imaginary one. Their exploitation of this fear—building societies—summer camps.

❖   ❖   ❖

Fourteenth anniversary of my Uncle's death. Fine. Cleaned the air-gun as usual. But what have I done to avenge, to disprove the boy's faked evidence at the inquest? NOTHING (never reloaded since it was found discharged beside your untasted coffee). Give me time. I PROMISE.

Only those in the last stage of disease could believe that children are true judges of character. The child's life is intermittent, isolated desultory jerks now and then, which scandalise and alarm its parents, but for the most part it is a motor run off their accumulators. My first memories of my Uncle were like images cast on the screen of a television set, maternally induced. My fascinated fear of his red sealing ring, his slightly protruding eyes with which he used to look at our house in a way that always made me feel ashamed of it. I could never make up my mind about their colour. Sometimes they seemed brown, sometimes blue, and sometimes a terrifying sea-green. I thought I hated him but I was always eager to please him or run errands, and a word of approval from him made me happy for the rest of the day.

He didn't come very often, but I can remember when I was about thirteen a letter from him coming at breakfast. 'Of course I know he's very clever', my mother sniffed, and then there was a silence.

It wasn't till I was sixteen and a half that he invited me to his flat. We had champagne for dinner. When I left I knew who and what he was—my real ancestor.

Dream Last Night.

I was on the bank of a deep river. On the further bank were B and a whole crowd standing round E who was tied to the rails of a railway track. An express was racing towards him. I knew that E was being executed on a charge of sabotage and that I had the evidence to save him if I could get there in time. Moored to the other bank was a ferry boat in which stood the ferryman, a tall fair young man whom I feel I have met before, but not in real life. His back was turned to me as he was watching the proceedings. Behind me a football match was in progress and the spectators were crying my name. I screamed to the ferryman, but their row drowned my voice completely. As the engine reached E the driver leant out with a disgusting leer, dangling a large old-fashioned fob and I saw the time was 6.0 a.m.

[47]

Everything disappeared as a newsboy touched my arm holding out a news-sheet bordered with black. At the top was a photograph of my Uncle Henry, the one which actually appeared at the time, but under it the words 'I have crossed it'. I woke hearing voices as if the battle were lost.

◇   ◇   ◇

Thursday.

The Hollies. Some blazers lounge beneath the calming tree; they talk in birds' hearing; girls come with roses, servants with a tray, skirting the sprinkler preaching madly to the grass, where mower worries in the afternoons. Draw not your leagues away, Too-much-alone.

Between box-edges, past the weathering urns, walk, acquire their ruses. Visit enough till coat-stand in their hall seem arsenal stocked against a life-time's harm.

These also dogs follow, are loved by grooms; milder than hawks have conquered fear of ledges, sailed over fishes swaying with the sea; have looked in ponds but not for reassurance; bathing in front of inattentive weasels, a tan-armed gonsil or a first-of-May.

O turn your head this way, be faithful here. The working mouth, the flimsy flexing knee, the leap in summer in the rubber shoes, these signal in their only codes. There is no other rendezvous for you to keep before the simple night (at night elopement is potty from the private drome. The little train will halt to pick up flowers). There are no other agents if these were cads. You stand in time's nick now with all to lose.

The spies have gone to phone for their police—locked behind mirrors in his study, his secret heroes ragging round the
fire, Death swots ungraceful, keen on his career; notes in his
journal 'I have never lived—left-handed and ironic, but have
loved'.

Again. Always the same weakness. No progress against this
terrible thing. What would E say if he knew? Dare I tell him?
Does Derek suspect? He looked at me very strangely at dinner.
No; no one must ever know. If the enemy ever got to hear
of it, my whole work would be nullified. I must be careful
to avoid sitting up with E alone to late hours. The signed
confession in my pocket shall remain unread, always.

A cold bath every morning. Never to funk but to return everything, no matter how distasteful the explanations. (The Hollies this evening, mind.) Whenever temptation is felt go at
once to do mechanical drawing.

Hands, in the name of my Uncle, I command you, or . . .

❖   ❖   ❖

Of the Enemy Gambits.

Hygiene against the awareness of likeness.

Newspapers against the awareness of difference.

To-day 'Seven-round contest against Worry. Distinguished
psychologist as referee'. On the football page—'Hearts hum-
bled by Queens'.

❖   ❖   ❖

The new batch of recruits arrived this morning, looking tired after the night journey but very excited about to-morrow. Poor little buggers. I'm afraid half of them won't get through the medical. Sands is too rough.

✦   ✦   ✦

There is something peculiarly horrible about the idea of women pilots.

✦   ✦   ✦

Derek was killed this afternoon. Went into a barrel roll at 8000 ft. and never came out. His collar bone was sticking through his navel. Of course the mechanics swear the machine was all right when it left the hangar, but I know better. When I saw the driver of that Renault wearing sphagnum moss in his cap, I ought to have realised. I ought never to have let him go up. Greath in March, Bronx last month, and now Derek. Yet B is still only half convinced.

✦   ✦   ✦

Enemy messages to be decoded—'The little apples will grow again.' 'Don't touch me or I'll spill.'

✦   ✦   ✦

Another awful night. Cabbage water very little good now. Waking early after night terrors. The faint tang of irretrievable disaster; as if Lake Constance were outside the window and had destroyed all countries and human beings. Solitude. Among the gooseberry bushes in the kitchen garden he crouches, scratched, holding his breath as the noisy steps approach. 'I bet he's here somewhere.' In the greenhouse they

[50]

loiter, imagine coiled shapes, malignant, phosphorescent, in the zinc darkness of a tank. Come on, you chaps! After their change of heart, a desert silence, shadows of wool-white clouds. A caterpillar, lacking compass or guides, crosses the vast uplands of his shoe, whom bees ignore. They have all gone in to tea. No one will look for you again.

Derek buried to-day. A choir of quarrymen and boys. Imagining one's death-bed; universal understanding and forgiveness; lines produced to meet at infinity; the eternised moment.

Conference at Arncliffe in the old water tower. B looking ill; Allen and Page like two rival railway companies—jealous and unaccommodating. Got Absalom through, but they still haggle about the cost of Lot's Wife (this operation is essential). Percy is not to be trusted and should be watched. The enemy's strength lies in the people's disbelief in his existence. If they believed he would be powerless. To convince them—unrelaxed attention—demonstration—sacred abuse.

Tea to-day at the Cardross Golf Club. A Hot-bed. Far too many monks in Sinclair Street.

There are some birds in these valleys
Who flutter round the careless
With intimate appeal,
By seeming kindness trained to snaring,
They feel no falseness.

Under the spell completely
They circle can serenely,
And in the tricky light
The masked hill has a purer greenness.
Their flight looks fleeter.

But fowlers, O, like foxes,
Lie ambushed in the rushes.
Along the harmless tracks
The madman keeper crawls through brushwood,
Axe under oxter.

Alas, the signal given,
Fingers on trigger tighten.
The real unlucky dove
Must smarting fall away from brightness
Its love from living.

◇   ◇   ◇

Of the Enemy's Definitions by Negation:
Unless you do well you will *not* be loved.
I'm *afraid* of death (instead of *I* want to live).
Pleasure is the *decrease* of pain (olives—whisky).

To him glory is only a reversal of rôle—the rejected lover's
phantasy—to be cold and to be desired, *e.g.* the Mimosa's
affair with the parachute jumper.

◇   ◇   ◇

Day-dreams of victory. Bomb fragment exposed by share, set
up on mantelpiece, a wonder to the new children. Renewal of
work at my monograph on Professional Jealousy. Aerial pho-
tography of earth-works in a harvest season.

Under the spell completely
They circle can serenely,
And in the tricky light
The masked hill has a purer greenness.
Their flight looks fleeter.

But fowlers, O, like foxes,
Lie ambushed in the rushes.
Along the harmless tracks
The madman keeper crawls through brushwood,
Axe under oxter.

Alas, the signal given,
Fingers on trigger tighten.
The real unlucky dove
Must smarting fall away from brightness
Its love from living.

Of the Enemy's Definitions by Negation:
Unless you do well you will *not* be loved.
I'm *afraid* of death (instead of *I* want to live).
Pleasure is the *decrease* of pain (olives—whisky).

To him glory is only a reversal of rôle—the rejected lover's
phantasy—to be cold and to be desired, *e.g.* the Mimosa's
affair with the parachute jumper.

Day-dreams of victory. Bomb fragment exposed by share, set
up on mantelpiece, a wonder to the new children. Renewal of
work at my monograph on Professional Jealousy. Aerial pho-
tography of earth-works in a harvest season.

loiter, imagine coiled shapes, malignant, phosphorescent, in the zinc darkness of a tank. Come on, you chaps! After their change of heart, a desert silence, shadows of wool-white clouds. A caterpillar, lacking compass or guides, crosses the vast uplands of his shoe, whom bees ignore. They have all gone in to tea. No one will look for you again.

Derek buried to-day. A choir of quarrymen and boys. Imagining one's death-bed; universal understanding and forgiveness; lines produced to meet at infinity; the eternised moment.

❖　❖　❖

Conference at Arncliffe in the old water tower. B looking ill; Allen and Page like two rival railway companies—jealous and unaccommodating. Got Absalom through, but they still haggle about the cost of Lot's Wife (this operation is essential). Percy is not to be trusted and should be watched. The enemy's strength lies in the people's disbelief in his existence. If they believed he would be powerless. To convince them—unrelaxed attention—demonstration—sacred abuse.

❖　❖　❖

Tea to-day at the Cardross Golf Club. A Hot-bed. Far too many monks in Sinclair Street.

❖　❖　❖

There are some birds in these valleys
Who flutter round the careless
With intimate appeal,
By seeming kindness trained to snaring,
They feel no falseness.

[51]

In hours of gentleness always to remember my Uncle, the connection between the last desperate appeals of the lost for help scribbled on the walls of public latrines and such a letter as this.

'The wound is healing and we can now look back to the war, not forgetting a sacrifice, and all the miseries which it caused, but without such very painful memories.

'Some people say "Why does anyone want to think about war at all?" and accuse those who do of militarist ideas. We weren't thinking about war in 1914, except for a small body of thinking soldiers and statesmen, who saw it inevitably approaching. The British nation as a whole had no thought or idea of war—and yet in a matter of days it was upon us, and, we entered it as thoughtlessly and light-heartedly as we would send off a team for a cricket match. I must say that the team —in this case the British Expeditionary Force—went into the game just as cheerfully and light-heartedly, if not more so— but that was their job as soldiers. The people who committed them to the greatest war in history, and who afterwards backed them up and took their turn so nobly, were the British public, the British nation.'

After Victory.

Few executions except for the newspaper peers—Viscount Stuford certainly. The Rev. McFarlane?
 Duchess of Holbrook for the new human zoo.
 Tom to have the Welsh Marches.
 Ian a choice of Durham and Norfolk.
 Edward for films.
 Gabriel to Foreign department.

B something he can't spoil.

Other posts to be decided as quickly as possible.

Monthly firework displays.

Much more research needed into the crucial problem—group organisation (the real parts).

♦ ♦ ♦

Very little progress this year. Never quite as bad as that dreadful spring of 1927, but still generally at week-ends. So much better when seeing E. The rose-bowl from Ardencaple still unreturned. Weak. Weak. Weak. No sooner do we succeed a little against the enemy than I let us all down, dishonour my Uncle. Look what happened after my fighting speech at Preston. Little did they guess when they chaired me what kind of a person it was to whom they were awarding that honour.

♦ ♦ ♦

August 23rd, 3 p.m.

We are lost. A cart has just passed carrying the plaster eagle. The enemy are going to attack.

♦ ♦ ♦

The enemy orders communicated to-night of August 23rd-24th—

1st Army: 15 attack divisions, 2 ordinary divisions.

2nd Army: 15 attack divisions, 3 ordinary divisions.

3rd Army: 19 attack divisions, 5 ordinary divisions.

Reserve: 3 attack divisions,

  To Norna, Dudley, Arno, Niagara—each a corps.

G.H.Q. Commands.

1. That the attack take place on Aug. 28th. First penetration of the hostile position, 7.10 a.m.
2. A feint landing by pleasure paddle-steamers near the bathing-machines on Beach V.
3. A flank attack in an E.N-E. direction by troops carrying special golf-ball grenades, to secure the heights above the club-house and to cut the York road.
4. A main frontal attack. Divisions to be concentrated in the Shenly brick-fields and moved forward to the battle zone in bakers' vans, disguised as nuns.
5. G.H.Q. retains command of 2nd Guard and 26th Nuthatchers.
6. Remaining Armies to act in accordance with the operation order 6925, dated July 26th.

First Day of Mobilisation.

At the pre-arranged zero hour the widow bent into a hoop with arthritis gives the signal for attack by unbending on the steps of St. Philip's. A preliminary bombardment by obscene telephone messages for not more than two hours destroys the *morale* already weakened by predictions of defeat made by wireless-controlled crows and card-packs. Shock troops equipped with wire-cutters, spanners and stink-bombs, penetrating the houses by infiltration, silence all alarm clocks, screw down the bathroom taps, and remove plugs and paper from the lavatories. The *Courier* Offices are the first objective. A leading article accusing prominent citizens of arson, barratry, coining, dozing in municipal offices, espionage, family skeletons, getting and bambling, heresy, issuing or causing to be issued false statements with intent to deceive, jingoism, keeping disorderly houses, mental cruelty, loitering, nepotism, onanism, piracy on the high seas, quixotry, romping at forbidden hours, sabotage, tea-drinking, unnatural offences against minors, vicious looks, will-burning, a yellow streak, is on the table of every householder in time for a late breakfast.

Conversion of hotels and boarding houses into private nursing-homes is carried out as rapidly as possible. Major operations without anaesthetics begin at noon. At 6 p.m. passages of unprepared translation from dead dialects are sent to all non-combatants. The papers are collected at 6.10. All who fail to obtain 99% make the supreme sacrifice. Candidates must write on three sides of the paper.

Second Day.

The nine o'clock business train leaves on a mystery trip through the more remote upland valleys; there is no refreshment car. Packed excursions at five-minute intervals, jumping the points, enter the sea from Craigendoran Pier. Slight modifications in the trams connecting the electric circuit with the seat buttons shrivel the lolling parcel-carriers. Banks make payments in fairy gold; girl-guides, nocturnally stimulated, mob vicars at the climax of their sermons; organists light pipes at the moment of consecration; at evensong choirs sing hymns in hesitation waltz time. Form-masters find crude graffiti on their blackboards; the boys, out of control, imbibe Vimto through india-rubber tubing, openly pee into the ink-pots.

A white-faced survivor informs the prison governor that the convicts, loosed, storming the execution shed, are calculating the drop formula by practical experiment, employing warders of varying weights.

Third Day.

Secret catalysts introduced into the city reservoirs convert the entire drinking supply into tepid urine. Adulterated milk drawn by order of the military from consumptive gentlewomen is only procurable by those who are fortunate enough to possess attractive daughters. The factories, structurally altered, reduce all raw products to an irritant filter-passing dust. Eyeballs of ravished virgins, black puddings made from the blood of the saints, sucking children already flyblown, are exposed for sale at famine prices. For those who desire an honourable release, typhoid lice, three in a box, price twopence, are peddled in the streets by starving corner boys.

Fourth Day.

All menstruation ceases. Vampires are common in the neighbourhood of the Cathedral, epidemics of lupus, halitosis, and superfluous hair.

Fifth Day.

Pressure of ice, falling fire. The last snarl of families beneath the toppling column. Biting at wounds as the sutures tear.

24th.

Four days. What's the use of counting them now?

25th.

Why, the words in my dream under Uncle's picture, 'I HAVE CROSSED IT.' To have been told the secret that will save everything and not to have listened; and now less than three days in which to prepare myself. My whole life has been mistaken, progressively more and more complicated, instead of finally simple.

My incredible blindness, with all the facts staring me in the face, not to have realised these elementary truths.

1. The power of the enemy is a function of our resistance, therefore
2. The only efficient way to destroy it—self-destruction, the sacrifice of all resistance, reducing him to the state of a man trying to walk on a frictionless surface.
3. Conquest can only proceed by absorption of, *i.e.* infection by, the conquered. The true significance of my hands. 'Do not imagine that you, no more than any other conqueror, escape the mark of grossness.' They stole to force a hearing.

To begin at once.

To my Uncle, perpetual gratitude and love for this crowning mercy. For myself, absolute humility.

I know that I am I, living in a small way in a temperate zone, blaming father, jealous of son, confined to a few acts often repeated, easily attracted to a limited class of physique, yet envying the simple life of the gut, desiring the certainty of the breast or prison, happiest sawing wood, only knowledge of the real, disturbances in the general law of the dream; the quick blood fretting against the slowness of the hope; a unit of life, needing water and salt, that looks for a sign.

What have I written? Thoughts suitable to a sanatorium. Three days to break a lifetime's pride.

26th.

Two days.
Read Mifflin on Air Currents.
A complete course for the commercial flying licence.
The life of Count Zeppelin (obtainable in Air and Airways
    Library).
Remember to pay Bryden's Bill.
To answer C's letter.
The £100 for Tom's holiday.
Destroy all letters, snapshots, lockets, etc., of E.
Further purification.
Deep breathing exercises instead of smoking.
A clean shirt, collar and handkerchief each morning till the
    end.

27th.

Supper at The Hollies. E alone. Salmon fresh from the loch. O understand, darling. God just loves us all, but means to be obeyed; and unaffecting is our solid tear. Thank you for your share in this, but good-bye. Uncle, save them all, make me worthy.

28th.

3.40 a.m.

        Pulses and reflexes, normal.
        Barometric reading, 30.6.
        Mean temperature, 34° F.,
        Fair. Some cumulus cloud at 10,000 feet.
           Wind easterly and moderate.
        Hands in perfect order.

BOOK III

FIVE ODES

I

WATCHING IN THREE PLANES from a
room overlooking the courtyard
That year decaying,
Stub-end of year that smoulders to ash of winter,
The last day dropping;
Lo, a dream met me in middle night, I saw in a vision
Life pass as a gull, as a spy, as a dog-hated dustman:
Heard a voice saying—'Savers, payers, payees, all of you,
Read of your losses.'

Shaped me a Lent scene first, a bed, hard, surgical,
And a wound hurting;
The hour in the night when Lawrence died and I came
Round from the morphia.
A train went clanking over the bridges leaving the city;
A sleep-walker pushed on groaning down the velvet passage;
The night-nurse visited—'We shall not all sleep, dearie,'
She said, and left me.

Felt sap collecting anon in unlighted cylinders
         For birdward facing;
The flat snake moving again in the pit, the schoolboy
         From home migrating.
After a night of storm was a lawn in sunlight,
A colleague bending for measurements there at the rain-gauge,
Gritting his teeth after breakfast, the Headmaster muttered
         'Call no man happy.'

Came summer like a flood, did never greediest gardener
         Make blossoms flusher:
Sunday meant lakes for many, a browner body
         Beauty from burning:
Far out in the water two heads discussed the position,
Out of the reeds like a fowl jumped an undressed German,
And Pretzel signalled from the sand dunes like a wooden
         madman
         'Destroy this temple.'

It did fall. The quick hare died to the hound's hot breathing,
         The Jewess fled Southwards;
The drunken Scotsman, regarding the moon's hedge-rising,
         Shook and saluted:
And in cold Europe, in the middle of Autumn destruction,
Maverick stood, his face grown lined with wincing
In front of ignorance—'Tell the English,' he shivered,
         'Man is a spirit.'

What I saw further was general but in sorrow,
         Many together
Forgiving each other in the dark of the picture palaces
         But past forgiveness;
The pair walking out on the mole, getting ready to quarrel,

The exile from superb Africa, employed in a laundry;
Deserters, mechanics, conjurers, delicate martyrs,
                    Yes, self-regarders.

I saw the brain-track perfected, laid for conveying
                    The fatal error,
Sending the body to islands or after its father,
                    Cold with a razor:
One sniffed at a root to make him dream of a woman,
One laid his hands on the heads of dear little pages;
Neither in the bed nor on the *arête* was there shown me
                    One with power.

'Save me!' the voice commanded, but as I paused hesitant,
                    A troop rushed forward
Of all the healers, granny in mittens, the Mop, the white
        surgeon,
                    And the suave archdeacon.
The captains grouped round the flagstaff shut up their glasses,
Broke yelping over the gravel—as I stood a spectator;
One tapped my shoulder and asked me 'How did you fall, sir?'
                    Whereat I awakened.

Roof-line sharpens, intense in the New Year morning;
                    Far down in courtyard
Beggar addresses the earth on the state of East Europe:
                    'Won't you speak louder?
Have you heard of someone swifter than Syrian horses?
Has he thrown the bully of Corinth in the sanded circle?
Has he crossed the Isthmus already? is he seeking brilliant
                    Athens and us?'

II

(To Edward Upward, Schoolmaster)

WHAT SIREN zooming is sounding our coming
Up frozen fjord forging from freedom?
What shepherd's call
When stranded on hill,
With broken axle
On track to exile?

With labelled luggage we alight at last
Joining joking at the junction on the moor
With practised smile
And harmless tale
Advance to meet
Each new recruit.

Expert from uplands, always in oilskins,
Recliner from library, laying down law,
Owner from shire,
All meet on this shore,

Facing each prick
With ginger pluck.

Our rooms are ready, the register signed,
There is time to take a turn before dark,
      See the blistering paint
      On the scorching front,
      Or icicles sombre
      On pierhead timber.

To climb the cliff path to the coastguard's point
Past the derelict dock deserted by rats,
      Look from concrete sill
      Of fort for sale
      To the bathers' rocks,
      The lovers' ricks.

Our boots will be brushed, our bolsters pummelled,
Cupboards are cleared for keeping our clothes.
      Here we shall live
      And somehow love,
      Though we only master
      The sad posture.

Picnics are promised and planned for July
To the wood with the waterfall, walks to find,
      Traces of birds,
      A mole, a rivet,
      In factory yards
      Marked strictly private.

There will be skating and curling at Christmas—indoors
Charades and ragging; then riders pass

Some afternoons
In snowy lanes,
Shut in by wires,
Surplus from wars.

In Spring we shall spade the soil on the border
For blooming of bulbs; we shall bow in Autumn,
When trees make passes
As high gale pushes,
And bewildered leaves
Fall on our lives.

We are here for our health, we have not to fear
The fiend in the furze or the face at the manse;
Proofed against shock,
Our hands can shake;
The flag at the golf-house flutters,
And nothing matters.

We shall never need another new outfit;
These grounds are for good, we shall grow no more.
But lose our colour,
With scurf on collar
Peering through glasses
At our own glosses.

This life is to last, when we leave we leave all,
Though vows have no virtue, though voice is in vain,
We live like ghouls
On posts from girls,
What the spirit utters
In formal letters.

Watching through windows the wastes of evening,
The flare of foundries at fall of the year,
The slight despair
At what we are,
The marginal grief
Is source of life.

In groups, forgetting the gun in the drawer,
Need pray for no pardon, are proud till recalled
By music on water
To lack of stature,
Saying Alas
To less and less.

Till holding our hats in our hands for talking
Or striding down streets for something to see,
Gas-light in shops,
The fate of ships,
And the tide-wind
Touch the old wound.

Till our nerves are numb and our now is a time
Too late for love or for lying either,
Grown used at last
To having lost,
Accepting dearth
The shadow of death.

III

(To John Warner, son of Rex and Frances Warner)

R oar Gloucestershire, do yourself proud;
The news I tell you should make you move
As a pride of lions or an exaltation of larks,
Not who you are but whom you foster
At Amberley near Stroud
Shall give you full marks.
I cannot state it too clearly, I shall not refrain,
It is John, son of Warner, has pulled my chain.

John Bull, John Bull, I understand well;
I know, Bull, I know what you want me to tell.
Calm, Bull, calm, news coming in time;
News coming, Bull; calm, Bull,
Fight it down, fight it down,
That terrible hunger; calm, Bull; first
We must have a look round, we must know the worst.

England our cow
Once was a lady—is she now?

Walk through her cities, walk with a pal
Through the streets between the power-house and green canal
And see what they're at—our proletariat.
O my, what peeps
At disheartened sweeps—
Fitters and moulders,
Wielders and welders,
Dyers and bakers
And boiler-tube makers,
Poofs and ponces,
All of them dunces.
Those over thirty,
Ugly and dirty,
What are they doing
Except just stewing?
Content for the year
With foods out of tins and very small beer—
Flaking the rust off obsolete plant,
Slacking at the corners, thinking 'I can't.'
Sloping up the hill, for they've nowhere else to go—
To the park and the platforms where the windbags blow,
Spying on athletes playing on a green,
Spying on kisses shown on a screen,
Their minds as pathic as a boxer's face,
Ashamed, uninteresting, and hopeless race.

As for our upper class:
Let's be frank a moment, fellows—they won't pass.
Majors, Vicars, Lawyers, Doctors, Advertisers, Maiden Aunts,
They're all in a funk but they daren't do a bunk,
Either rufflers or mousers, they haven't a chance.
'I shall have to be careful until I see,
But I'll like you if you'll love me.'

'Careful, careful; can we afford it?'
'Careful, careful; till we've insured it.'
'Careful, careful; don't kiss me please.
Don't you know there's such a thing as disease?'
'The Duchess of Atholl with a *lorgnette*
Is observing the dunes; we can't bathe yet.'
'If she or the Bishop of London caught us,
They'd be certain to report us.'
'Hush! not a word of the beast with two backs
Or Mead and Muskett will be on our tracks!'
Wakeful at night, in the morning fagged;
They feel like angels, but they look just shagged.
'Kind to their women, indeed too kind,
It's a pity their women go out of their mind.'

Who will save?
Who will teach us how to behave?

O yes, MacDonald's a giant,
President Hoover's a giant,
Baldwin and Briand are giants—
Haven't they told us?
But why have they sold us?
They said they were winners,
They were only beginners.
Pygmies, poor dears,
Beside the Giant Sloths and the Giant Despairs.
Mussolini, Pilsudski and Hitler have charm
But they make such a noise:
We're getting a little tired of boys,
Of the ninny, the mawmet and the false alarm.

These had stopped seeking
But went on speaking,

Have not contributed,
But have diluted.

These ordered light
But had no right,
And handed on
War and a son.

Wishing no harm
But to be warm
These went to sleep
On the burning heap.

Who will save?
Who will teach us how to behave?

'Youth's on the march' says Jocker to Prushun.
Youth's the solution of every good scout.
Youth has the secret Toc H has found out.
Youth's a success.
Youth has the blessing of the *Sunday Express*.
Youth, says the teacher.
Youth, says the bishop.
Youth, says the bumslapper.
'Strewth, says I,
They're most of them dummies who want their mummies,
In Rolls or on bicycle they bolt for mama,
Let them scorch as they like for they won't get far.
Look at them now,
Sooner or later it'll come to the pater,
Sooner or later there'll be a row.

Who'll save, who?
Who'll save John Bull

From losing his wool?
Now, Bull, now
I'll tell you who,
I'll tell you how
The flying stationer flies round the corner.
Here it is, look! John, son of Warner,
John, son of Warner, shall rescue you.

You awkward pairs in studios upstairs
Spending a secret hour in learning
The One-step, the Two-step, the Tango, the Blues,
Stumbling, tripping, practising, turning,
Aching, blushing, almost in tears,
Relax completely now at my news:
A different teacher is born to this nation;
He'll teach you deportment and co-ordination.
Because of this boy
You shall dance without difficulty, you shall dance for joy.

A birthday, yes, a day without rain,
A cake but no candles, we're born again;
The church cat is ordering cocktail glasses,
The general's arranging the ensemble classes,
The cissy is going for cross-country runs,
We haven't much time, get ready at once
For John
Goal-getter, holer-in-one,
Hurdler, high-jumper, hope of our side,
Our hush-hush engine, our wonder liner,
Our gadget, our pride,
Our steel-piercing bullet, our burglar-proof safe,
Will
Save.

Wanted by John: —
Brains and nerve,
Some for shock-troops, some for reserve,
For propaganda, for section-commander,
For transport, dispatches—there're posts to fill.
The son from the bungalow up the hill
With the crazy paving and the squash-court,
He shall report.
The girl from Ivydene if she's alive,
Descend its dreary drive.
To-day may mean division for the newly-weds,
To-day although American Pillar
Fertilize Dorothy Perkins and kill her,
Rose-lovers also must leave their beds,
Caddies and kiddies leave colonel and kitchen
For John, son of Warner, shall find you your pigeon.

Spring again,
In the buds, in the birds, in the bowels, and the brain,
Spring in the bedroom ventilator,
Spring in the bearing of the hotel waiter;
At every corner
News of Warner,
His march on London,
His enemies undone.

Now Cods the curate coughs in the church,
With Ballocks the rector he's left in the lurch.
In the neo-Tudor club-house the captains frown,
The poor old colonel is red to the ears
'Phoning the Army and Navy for chairs
(He's only got a bayonet and he wants to sit down).

Dear me! Where is that darling dreamer,
That piss-proud prophet, that pooty redeemer,
The bigger magician with his Polish lad,
The aesthetic, the ascetic, the malicious and the mad?
Wouldn't they like to stop the cheering—
Hearing the arrival of his special train,
Hearing the fireworks, the saluting and the guns—
Bob and Miss Belmairs spooning in Spain?
Where is the trained eye? Under the sofa.
Where is Moxon? Dreaming of nuns.
Their day is over, they shall decorate the Zoo
With Professor Jeans and Bishop Barnes at 2d a view,
Or be ducked in a gletcher, as they ought to be,
With the Simonites, the Mosleyites and the I.L.P.

Queer to these birds: yes, very queer,
But to the tryers such a dear,
Only hard
On smugging, smartness, and self-regard,
See him take off his coat and get down with a spanner
To each unhappy Joseph and repressed Diana,
Say Bo to the invalids and take away their rugs,
The war-memorials decorate with member-mugs,
The gauche and the lonely he will introduce of course
To the smaller group, the right field of force;
The few shall be taught who want to understand,
Most of the rest shall love upon the land;
Living in one place with a satisfied face
All of the women and most of the men
Shall work with their hands and not think again.

This is the season of the change of heart,
The final keeping of the ever-broken vow,

The official re-marriage of the whole and part,
The poor in employment and the country sound,
Over is the tension, over the alarms,
The falling wage, and the flight from the pound,
The privates are returning now to the farms,
The silo is full, the marsh under plough,
The two worlds in each other's arms.
Falcon is poised over fell in the cool,
Salmon draws
Its lovely quarrons through the pool.
A birthday, a birth
On English earth
Restores, restore will, has restored
To England's story
The directed calm, the actual glory.

IV

(To My Pupils)

Though aware of our rank and alert to obey orders,
Watching with binoculars the movement of the grass for
an ambush,
The pistol cocked, the code-word committed to memory,
The youngest drummer
Knows all the peace-time stories like the oldest soldier,
Though frontier-conscious.

About the tall white gods who landed from their open boat,
Skilled in the working of copper, appointing our feast-days,
Before the islands were submerged, when the weather was
calm,
The maned lion common,
An open wishing-well in every garden;
When love came easy.

Perfectly certain, all of us, but not from the records,
Not from the unshaven agent who returned to the camp;

The pillar dug from the desert recorded only
                    The sack of a city,
The agent clutching his side collapsed at our feet,
                    'Sorry! They got me!'

Yes, they were living here once but do not now,
Yes, they are living still but do not here;
Lying awake after Lights Out a recruit may speak up:
                    'Who told you all this?'
The tent-talk pauses a little till a veteran answers
                    'Go to sleep, Sonny!'

Turning over he closes his eyes, and then in a moment
Sees the sun at midnight bright over cornfield and pasture,
Our hope. . . . Someone jostles him, fumbling for boots,
                    Time to change guard:
Boy, the quarrel was before your time, the aggressor
                    No one you know.

Your childish moments of awareness were all of our world,
At five you sprang, already a tiger in the garden,
At night your mother taught you to pray for our Daddy
                    Far away fighting,
One morning you fell off a horse and your brother mocked you:
                    'Just like a girl!'

Now we're due to parade on the square in front of the
          Cathedral,
When the bishop has blessed us, to file in after the choir-boys,
To stand with the wine-dark conquerors in the roped-off pews,
                    Shout ourselves hoarse:
'They ran like hares; we have broken them up like firewood;
                    They fought against God.'

[79]

While in a great rift in the limestone miles away
At the same hour they gather, tethering their horses beside
    them;
A scarecrow prophet from a boulder foresees our judgment,
              Their oppressors howling;
And the bitter psalm is caught by the gale from the rocks:
            'How long shall they flourish?'

What have we all been doing to have made from Fear
That laconic war-bitten captain addressing them now?
'Heart and head shall be keener, mood the more
          As our might lessens':
To have caused their shout 'We will fight till we lie down
    beside
          The Lord we have loved.'

There's Wrath who has learnt every trick of guerilla warfare,
The shamming dead, the night-raid, the feinted retreat;
Envy, their brilliant pamphleteer, to lying
         As husband true,
Expert Impersonator and linguist, proud of his power
        To hoodwink sentries;

Gluttony living alone, austerer than us,
Big simple greed; Acedia famed with them all
For her stamina, keeping the outposts; and somewhere Lust
        With his sapper's skill,
Muttering to his fuses in a tunnel 'Could I meet here with Love,
        I would hug him to death.'

There are faces there for which for a very long time
We've been on the look-out, though often at home we
    imagined,

Catching sight of a back or hearing a voice through a
    doorway,
            We had found them at last;
Put our arms round their necks and looked in their eyes and
    discovered
            We were unlucky.

And some of them, surely, we seem to have seen before:
Why, that girl who rode off on her bicycle one fine summer
    evening
And never returned, she's there; and the banker we'd noticed
            Worried for weeks,
Till he failed to arrive one morning and his room was empty,
            Gone with a suitcase.

They speak of things done on the frontier we were never told,
The hidden path to their squat Pictish tower
They will never reveal though kept without sleep, for their
    code is
            'Death to the squealer':
They are brave, yes, though our newspapers mention their
    bravery
            In inverted commas.

But careful; back to our lines; it is unsafe there;
Passports are issued no longer; that area is closed;
There's no fire in the waiting-room now at the climber's
    Junction,
            And all this year
Work has been stopped on the power-house; the wind whistles
    under
            The half-built culverts.

All leave is cancelled to-night; we must say good-bye;
We entrain at once for the North; we shall see in the morning
The headlands we're doomed to attack; snow down to the tide-
    line:
                Though the bunting signals
'Indoors before it's too late; cut peat for your fires,'
          We shall lie out there.

V

Not, father, further do prolong
   Our necessary defeat;
Spare us the numbing zero-hour,
   The desert-long retreat.

Against your direct light, displayed,
   Regardant, absolute,
In person stubborn and oblique
   We set our maddened foot.

These nissen huts if hiding could
   Your eye inseeing from,
Firm fenders were, but look! to us
   Your loosened angers come.

Against your accusations
   Though ready wit devise,
Nor magic countersigns prevail
   Nor airy sacrifice.

Weaker we are, and strict within
  Your organised blockade,
And from our desperate shore the last
  Few pallid youngsters fade.

Be not another than our hope;
  Expect we routed shall
Upon your peace; with ray disarm,
  Illumine, and not kill.

Epilogue

'OWHERE ARE YOU GOING?' said reader to rider,
'That valley is fatal when furnaces burn,
Yonder's the midden whose odours will madden,
That gap is the grave where the tall return.'

'O do you imagine,' said fearer to farer,
'That dusk will delay on your path to the pass,
Your diligent looking discover the lacking
Your footsteps feel from granite to grass?'

'O what was that bird,' said horror to hearer,
'Did you see that shape in the twisted trees?
Behind you swiftly the figure comes softly,
The spot on your skin is a shocking disease.'

'Out of this house'—said rider to reader
'Yours never will'—said farer to fearer
'They're looking for you'—said hearer to horror
As he left them there, as he left them there.

ABOUT THE AUTHOR

WYSTAN HUGH AUDEN was born in York, England, in 1907. He has been a resident of the United States since 1939, and an American citizen since 1946. Educated at Gresham's School, Holt, and at Christ Church, Oxford, he became associated with a small group of young writers in London—among them Stephen Spender and Christopher Isherwood—who became recognized as the most promising of the new generation in English letters. He collaborated with Isherwood on several plays, among them THE DOG BENEATH THE SKIN *and* THE ASCENT OF F-6 *(available as* TWO GREAT PLAYS *in Vintage Books).*

Mr. Auden is the author of several volumes of poetry, including ABOUT THE HOUSE, HOMAGE TO CLIO, THE DOUBLE MAN, FOR THE TIME BEING, THE AGE OF ANXIETY, NONES, *and* THE SHIELD OF ACHILLES. *His* SELECTED POETRY *appears in The Modern Library.* THE ENCHAFÈD FLOOD, *three critical essays on the romantic spirit, is available in Vintage Books. A volume of essays,* THE DYER'S HAND, *appeared in 1962. A new edition of* COLLECTED SHORTER POEMS *was published in 1967.*

Mr. Auden has been the recipient of a number of awards, among them the Pulitzer Prize, the National Book Award, the Bollingen Prize for Poetry, the Guinness Poetry Award and, in 1967, the National Medal for Literature given by the National Book Committee.